Warm summers and mild winters with close proximity to the Mediterranean Sea give this seaside city charismatic charm. Love of originality and raw beauty is visible in the city's architecture, music, cuisine and performance art, and the city is populated by people with a passion for food and living. Innovation is an essential part of life, and small shops, bars, designers and creative types bring constant new ideas to the table. To get to know the real flavour of Barcelona, bring a similarly open mind and warm heart.

CITIx60: Barcelona explores the Catalan capital and the second largest city of Spain in five aspects, covering architecture, art spaces, shops and markets, eating and entertainment. With expert advice from 60 stars of the city's creative scene, this book guides you to the real attracti_____e of Barcelona life.

Contents

Before You Go

BASIC INFO

Currency
Euro (EUR/€)
Exchange rate: €1 : $1.4

Time zone
GMT +1
DST +2

DST begins at 0200 (local time) on the last Sunday of March and ends at 0300 (local time) on the last Sunday of October.

Dialling
International calling: +34
Citywide: 93

Weather (avg. temperature range)
Spring (Mar–May): 10–19°C / 50–66°F
Summer (Jun–Sep): 20–28°C / 68–82°F
Autumn (Oct–Nov): 12–20°C / 54–68°F
Winter (Dec–Feb): 5–14°C / 41–57°F

USEFUL WEBSITES

Citywide public transport advisor
www.tmb.cat/en

Pocket Wifi
www.wifivox.com

EMERGENCY CALLS

Ambulance / Fire
061 / 080

Police
092

Embassies / consulates
China   +34 93 25 41 199
Japan   +34 93 28 03 433
France   +34 93 27 03 000
Germany   +34 93 29 21 000
UK   +34 90 21 09 356
US   +34 93 28 02 227

AIRPORT EXPRESS TRANSFER

El Prat <-> Passeig de Gràcia
Trains / Journey: every 30 min / 25 min
From Aeropuerto or Passeig de Gràcia Station (Gràcia) – 0600-2330
One-way: €3 or less than €1 with T10
www.renfe.com

El Prat (T1) <-> pl. Catalunya (Aerobús A1)
Bus / Journey: every 5-10 min / 35 min
From El Prat – 0610-0105
From Plaza Catalunya – 0530-0030
One-way: €5.90
www.aerobusbcn.com

PUBLIC TRANSPORT IN BARCELONA

Metro
Bus & NitBus
Train
Tram
Taxi
Funicular

Means of Payment
T10 Travel card*
Credit cards (Metro ticket vending machine)
Cash

*Each trip includes three bus, metro, train or tramway transfers made within 75 min.

BANK HOLIDAYS

January	1 New Year's Day, 6 Epiphany
March/April	Good Friday, Easter Monday
May	1 Labour Day
May/June	Whit Monday
June	24 Saint Joan
August	15 Assumption Day
September	11 Diada
October	12 Columbus Day
November	1 All Saints' Day
December	8 Immaculate Conception, 25 Christmas Day

Cultural institutions and shops might be closed or have varied opening hours on public holidays.

FESTIVALS / EVENTS

January
080 Barcelona Fashion (also in July)
www.080barcelonafashion.cat

March
Mutek
www.mutek.org

May
LOOP Barcelona
www.loop-barcelona.com
OFFF Barcelona
www.offf.ws
Primavera Sound
www.primaverasound.es

June
Barcelona Design Week
www.barcelonadesignweek.com
Piknic Electronik
piknicelectronik.es
Pride Barcelona
www.pridebarcelona.org
Sónar
www.sonar.es
Swab
swab.es

August / September
Festa Major de Gràcia
www.festamajordegracia.cat
Festes de la Mercè
www.spanish-fiestas.com

October / November
Barcelona Jazz festival
www.barcelonajazzfestival.com
L'Alternativa Film Festival
www.alternativa.cccb.org
WeArt Festival
www.weartfestival.com

December
Festivalet
www.festivalet.org

Event days vary by year. Please check for updates online.

UNUSUAL OUTINGS

Barcelona Architecture Walks
www.barcelonarchitecturewalks.com

Culinary Backstreets
www.culinarybackstreets.com

Hidden City Tours
hiddencitytours.com

My Favourite Things
www.myft.net

Rainbow Barcelona Tours
rainbowbarcelona.es

Ride or Die Bike Rental and Tours
www.rideordie.es

SMARTPHONE APP

Hidden spots discovered
BCN Paisatge

Public transport in control
TMB Virtual

Bike routes, locator & available bikes/docks
CityBikeApp

REGULAR EXPENSES

Single public transport ticket
€2

Domestic / International mail (postcards)
€0.75 / €0.90

Gratuities
Diners: optional 5% for waitstaff & round up to whole amount bartenders
Hotels: €1@bag for the porter, €1 daily for cleaners
Licensed taxis: €1-2

*Look out for pickpockets. They find targets in subways or come on bicycles.

Count to 10

What makes Barcelona so special?
Illustrations by Guillaume Kashima aka Funny Fun

Life in Barcelona is a rich tapestry of traditions and tastes brimming with creativity. Niche magazines, artisanal food and drink, modernist architecture and contemporary art thrives, making the trend-ready city a pleasure for the senses. Whether you are on a one-day stopover or a week-long stay, see what Barcelona creatives consider essential to see, taste, read and take home from your trip.

1

Architecture

Eixample (#3)
by Ildefons Cerdà

La Sagrada Familia (#9)
by Antoni Gaudí

Santa Maria del mar Church
by Berenguer de Montagu

Palau Baró de Quadras
by Josep Puig i Cadafalch

Palau de la Música Catalana
by Lluís Doménech i Montaner

Parc dels Auditoris
by Jacques Herzog, Pierre de Meuron & the International Convention Centre of Barcelona

Torre Diagonal Zero Zero
by EMBA

2

Parks

Poblenou Park
by Jean Nouvel
Av. Diagonal 130, El Poblenou

Parc Güell (#12)
by Antoni Gaudí
c/Olot 5, El Carmel

Parc del Laberint d'Horta
18th century Labyrinth Park
by Domenico Bagutti
Pg. Castanyers 1, Horta

Parc de la Ciutadella (#5)
by Josep Fontseré
Pg. Picasso 21, La Ribera

Parc de L'Espanya Industrial
by Luis Peña Ganchegui
c/Muntadas 1-37, Sants

**Cactus Garden
(Parc de Montjuïc)**
*c/Doctor Font i Quer 2,
Parc de Montjuïc*

3

Nourishments

Botifarra (sausage)
Botifarrería de Santa María
c/Santa María 4, La Ribera

Calçots (scallion)
La Masia de Can Portell
www.lamasiacanportell.com

**Patatas bravas
(fried potatoes)**
Samsara
c/Terol 6, Vila de Gràcia

Paella
Cheriff
c/Ginebra 15, La Barceloneta

**Xocolata amb xurros
(chocolate with churros)**
c/Petrixol, El Gòtic

4

Local Brews,
Wines & Spirits

Serpis by La Fée Verte
La Cava de los Faros
www.spiritscorner.com

Voll-Damm
Murray Bagel Shop
www.murraysbagels.com

Moritz
Fàbrica Moritz Barcelona (#47)
www.moritz.com

Homemade vermouth
Morro Fi (#52)
or bodega Costa Brava
c/Alzina 58, Vila de Gràcia

Vermouth & wine
Casa Mariol
www.casamariol.com

Wine from Priorat
Vila Viniteca
www.vilaviniteca.es

8

Markets

Mercat del Ninot
Fresh produce & Jabugo ham
www.mercatdelninot.com

Lost&found Barcelona
Secondhand market
lostfoundmarket.com

Mercat de Sant Antoni
Odds & ends
www.mercatdesantantoni.com

SusiSweetdress Market
Vintage dresses
www.susisweetdress.com

Mercat del Clot
Bizarre souvenir
www.mercatdelclot.net

Els Encants Vells (#10)
www.encantsbcn.com

Mercat de la Boquería (#36)
www.boqueria.info

9

Mementos

Catalan designer clothes
by Antonio Miró or Sita Murt

**A Marquina 1961 Olive Oil Cruet
& a Krasznai ceramic**
Vinçon (#34)

Porró (wine pitcher)
Mercat Accessible
c/Rosselló 495, Sagrada Familia

Traditional Catanlan espadrilles
La Manual Alpargatera
lamanualalpargatera.es

A Cobi figure
El Coleccionista
c/Enric Granados 102 , L'Eixample

Olive oil (Siurana origin)
Oro Líquido
www.oroliquido.es

10

Leisure

Beach Picnic
Nova Icaria / Bogatell

**Longboard skating
around the city**
Inercia Shop
www.inercia-shop.com

Explore the city
Bike along coastal line
from W Hotel to Parc del Fòrum

See the Castellers
pl. Sant Jaume, El Gòtic

Eat ice cream in summer
Gelateria Italiana
Pl. de la Revolució, Vila de Gràcia

A walk around Montjuïc
See Castell de Montjuïc, The
Olympic Ring, Botanical Gardens,
Cementiri de Montjuïc

Icon Index

 Opening hours

 Admission

 Address

 Facebook

 Contact

 Website

 Remarks

 Scan QR codes to access Google Maps and discover the area around each destination. Internet connection required.

60x60

60 Local Creatives x 60 Hotspots

From vast cityscapes to the smallest snippets of conversation, there is much to inspire creative urges in Barcelona. 60x60 points you to 60 haunts where 60 arbiters of taste develop their nose for the good stuff.

Landmarks & Architecture   SPOTS · 01 – 12 📍

Experience a charming blend of old with new. Start at Eixample to tour *modernista* architecture before taking a ramble to the labyrinth old town.

Cultural & Art Space   SPOTS · 13 – 24 📍

Be inspired by the dynamic melting pot of artistic disciplines, from movement to sound arts. Creative spaces and art factories offer cultural programmes all day long.

Markets & Shops   SPOTS · 25 – 36 📍

Let independent boutiques and century-old family businesses greet you with proud selections, then find Catalan wine and choice food at groceries and markets.

Restaurants & Cafés   SPOTS · 37 – 48 📍

Start your day with a pre-lunch vermouth before hitting the famed tapas – rich cacophonies of tasty small dishes. Don't miss traditional Catalan stews and sauces.

Nightlife   SPOTS · 49 – 60 📍

Bask in Barcelona's sunset on a high ground, then go bar-hopping or watch a play after dark. Pubs and bars offer roots, reggae, soul, techno, flamenco and Spanish Copla, among others.

Landmarks & Architecture

Catalan modernism, new architecture and Barcelona's skyline

Barcelona's distinctive architecture offers an ideal way to contemplate the city. Although new designs like Torre Agbar by Jean Nouvel and Els Encants Vells (#10) by local practice b720 are slowly transforming Barcelona's skyline, churches, mansions and factories from the 19th and 20th century remain a main attraction of this landscape. La Sagrada Familia (#9) by Antoni Gaudí, still an incomplete construction after 130 years, and Ildefons Cerdà's visionary Eixample grid street plan (#3) are icons and cannot be missed, but sniff out more hidden treasures, around the neighbouring districts, including el Gòtic, el Born, el Raval, Vila de Gràcia (#2) and Sant Antoni, and the earlier works of Gaudí at El Dipòsit de les Aigües (#1) and Parc de la Ciutadella (#5). If you have only one day, take the "Modernist Route (map D)" to track down the most iconic examples of Catalan Modernism, such as Casa Batlló and Casa Milà (also known as 'La Pedrera') both Gaudí masterpieces, and other works by Josep Puig i Cadafalch and Lluís Doménech i Montaner.

Albert Ibanyez
Graphic designer

Born in Barcelona, currently working freelance on projects related to art, editorial, typography and web design with clients like Fundació Antoni Tàpies and ELISAVA.

Dipòsit de les Aigües
P.014

Vila de Gràcia
P.015

Carles Enrich Giménez
Architect & interior designer

I combine research, teaching and practice in my own studio and develop alternative ways to unify houses with the city. I like to see architecture with a multidisciplinary look.

CrousCalogero
Design agency

A Barcelona-based consultancy founded in 2009 by Francesc Crous and Alessandro Calogero who met at the Innovation Lab at Roca. We are also professors at EINA Barcelona.

Eixample
P.016

Enric Soldevila
Creative director, TBWA Amsterdam

I worked as a 3D artist, graphic designer, art director and teacher. I did an around-the-world trip with a stop in the Tokyo jail and love to ride my motorbike as fast as I can.

Bunker del Carmel
P.017

Parc de la Ciutadella
P.018

Karlota Laspalas
Fashion designer

Fashion designer born in Pamplona, 1981. My work is a constant observation and experimentation of human identity, exploring our fears, longings and hopes.

Isa Rodríguez
Founder, INDASTUDIO BCN

Interior designer and creative director of INDASTUDIO BCN. Graduated from Bau Design College and previously worked with Sandra Taruella and Isabel López.

Disseny HUB Barcelona
P.019

Max-o-matic
Designer & illustrator

I'm Máximo Tuja, a collage artist and fanzine lover based in Barcelona since 2002. In my spare time I play with my son, run middle distances and make (horrible) music with friends.

Carretera de les Aigües
P.020

Pavelló Mies Van Der Rohe
P.021

Isahac Oliver Ponce
Creative director, &Rosàs

I'm 35 years old, married and a brand new father. I have been working in advertising for 13 years and right now am the executive creative director of new advertising adventure, &Rosàs.

Frank Plant
Artist

I'm an American sculptor based in Barcelona for 14 years. I do drawings in steel plate and bar that observe objects and social dynamics.

La Sagrada Familia
P.022

Borja Martínez
Founder, Lo Siento

My name is Borja Martínez, founder of Lo Siento studio in Barcelona. Our projects are mainly related to culture, music and food. We love to eat and take humour very seriously.

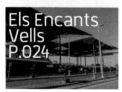

Els Encants Vells
P.024

La Barceloneta
P.025

Atipus
Graphic design studio

We are a Barcelona-based studio founded in 1998, working across a variety of media and fields. We believe in conceptual, creative and simple design.

UnitedFakes
Multimedia design studio

We are a multidisciplinary team who likes to switch roles in every project. As much as we use computers daily, we still love to get our hands dirty.

Parc Güell
P.028

1 Dipòsit de les Aigües
Map F, P.108

Sitting discreetly inside Universitat Pompeu Fabra's Ciutadella's campus is "The Water Tank," the university's main library. Its name originates from the site's earlier incarnation as a reservoir for Parc de la Ciutadella's (#5) cascade and irrigation, a Joseph Fontserè project on which Antoni Gaudí (1852-1926) assisted as a student architect in 1876. Said to be a copy of Italy's Piscina Mirabilis but with pool built on the rooftop, the building is now a fortified hypostyle hall accommodating a rich book collection and study areas comprising 7,850sqm. Enter through the entrance at the adjacent Jaume I block, the library is open to all visitors.

🕐 0800-0100 (M-F), 1000-2100 (Sa-Su, & P.H.) 🏠 Ramon Trias Fargas, 25-27, Vila Olimpica URL www.upf.edu/campus/en/ciutadella/aigues.html

"In the university's cafeteria there are sandwiches for €1 and coffee for 50 cents."

– Albert Ibanyez

2 Vila de Gràcia

Map D, P.104

Vila de Gràcia is a hipster barrio buzzing with the yesteryear charm of an older independent municipality. In between the area's low-rise buildings, roughly bounded by avinguda Diagonal to its south, find character shops like Duduá and BOO. Hit bars and terraces along carrer de Verdi or visit Bodega Bonavista at carrer de Bonavista 10 for local artisanal beers and Catalan wines. If you come in late August, be sure to join "Festes Major," where decoration, live music, pyrotechnics and cultural entertainment fill the streets.

 Duduá: duduadudua.com, BOO: www.boobcn.com, La Festes Gràcia: www. festamajordegracia.cat

"*Take a walk through the small squares in the dense 19th century urban structures across from plaça de la Vila, the Central Market or plaça de la Virreina.*"

– Carles Enrich Giménez

3 Eixample

Map K, P.111

If you're coming in by air, the most notice-able feature looking down is the city centre's extensive grid pattern, which urban planner Ildefons Cerdà (1815-76) drew up more than 150 years ago. Cerdà's gift for Barcelona's people were broad streets and square blocks with chamfered corners allowing considerable sunlight, high visibility and ventilation in the extended space – a blessing for townsfolk that had been packed into an overcrowded city experiencing rapid population growth. The area is known today as Eixample, which is Catalan for "extension."

URL Any Cerdà: www.anycerda.org
On the days Tibidabo Park operates, Tibibus T2A/B take visitors to the peak from pl. Catalunya or Sant Genís, www.tibidabo.cat

"Find the best view of Barcelona at the Tibidabo Park."
– CrousCalogero

4 Bunker del Carmel

Map C, P.103

Once the core of Barcelona's defences against 1936–9 fascist aerial attacks, the Spanish Civil War bunker is now a hush-hush spot to savour the city. Enjoy a picnic, with music, friends or loved ones, or just soak up the sun from this lofty point in the hilly neighbourhood of Carmel. Moving up one of the steepest slopes in Barcelona, however, requires some strength. Take a 30-minute walk uphill from Guinardó Station (L4), or take bus 119 from El Coll Station (L5) uphill and find the little path that leads to the top.

🏠 *c/Marià Lavernia 59, el Carmel*

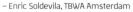

"In the 1950s, many Spanish immigrants built their houses here which developed into barracas (favela). Now you can find the best views of the city here."

– Enric Soldevila, TBWA Amsterdam

5 Parc de la Ciutadella
Map F, P.108

Take a break from the city with a leisurely picnic on the parterre or row a boat among wild geese and ducks in the great lake. Beautifully landscaped in 1872 by Josep Fontseré (1829–97) for the bourgeoisie, Ciutadella Park distinguishes itself with numerous Catalan sculptures, the lake, fountains, rich vegetation and architecture. Central to the design is the Baroque Cascade, alongside the shade house, the Greenhouse and a turreted castle created for the Universal Exhibition in 1888. The park is also home to the Parliament of Catalonia and Barcelona Zoo, to its south.

🕐 1000 till dusk daily
📍 pg. Picasso 21, la Ribera
🔗 Zoo: €19.90/11.95/10.05

"Enjoy a pleasant walk admiring wonderful buildings, fountains and lakes designed by architects as important as Domenech i Montaner and Gaudí."

– Karlota Laspalas

6 Disseny HUB Barcelona (DHUB)
Map B, P.102

The city's new design centre emphasises public space as much as an area to display design works. In contrast to the Jean Nouvel-designed Torre Agbar at Plaça de les Glòries, the zinc-clad angular edifice houses an auditorium and temporary exhibition halls over seven floors, and extends underground to host the main exhibition hall, a public library, restaurants and main offices, all lit by skylight. Design HUB Barcelona (DHUB) intends to exhibit far-reaching programmes across fashion, graphics, space and product design.

🕙 1600-2030 (M), 1000- (Tu-Su)
🏠 pl. de les Glòries Catalanes 37-38, el Parc i la Llacuna del Poblenou ☎ +34 93 25 66 700
URL www.dissenyhubbarcelona.cat

"Stroll around the outside space with its lake and ground lighting effects, then visit the Agbar Tower and the new Encants Market (#10)."

– Isa Rodríguez, INDASTUDIO BCN

7 Carretera de les Aigües
Map K, P.111

Sitting in the hills of Collserola, Carretera de
les Aigües is a wide, flat unpaved path, where
water pipes used to run. With spectacular
views of Barcelona and its coastline, the track
is a natural hot spot for a morning jog or bike
ride with fresh air and zero cars. Access the
trail by taking FGC (S1/S2) to Peu del Funicular,
then change to the Vallvidrera line and alight at
Carretera de les Aigües station. If you are keen
to walk, the meandering path will guide you to
Tibidabo, though it gets much steeper near the
hilltop. Those avoiding the climb should leave
at pla dels Maduixers and return to the city
through avinguda Tibidabo.

*"If you have your running shoes with you, put them
on and go there. You have about 20km to train for
your next race or just to disconnect from everything."*

– Máximo Tuja aka Max-o-matic

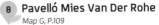

8 Pavelló Mies Van Der Rohe

Map G, P.109

Erected for the 1929 Barcelona International Exhibition, the German Pavilion by Ludwig Mies van der Rohe (1886–1969) portrayed the new Germany as a prospering democratic country, with an open plan, proportional interplay between interior and exterior space, reflection and actuality, the man-made and the natural. The infamous Barcelona Chair was also created as part of the design. The original pavilion, however, was removed in 1930 after the fair's closure, and was only rebuilt in 1986.

🕐 1000–2000 daily 💲 €5/2.60
🏠 av. Francesc Ferrer i Guàrdia 7, La Font de la Guatlla, Montjuïc
📞 +34 93 42 34 016
URL www.miesbcn.com
🔗 Guided tour: 1000–1200 (Sa)

"Near Montjuïc you can admire this 20th century landmark, a result of the painstaking reconstruction carried out in the 1980s."

– Isahac Oliver Ponce, &Rosàs

9 La Sagrada Família

Map D, P.105

Since 1883, the church of La Sagrada Família
has been a grand work in progress. Architect
Antoni Gaudí (1852–1926), a religious man with
a love for nature, had envisaged the design a
catechistic explanation of the teachings of the
Gospels and the Church. Complex structures
loaded with symbolic details were planned,
including many parts that the architect knew
he would not live to see built. In fact, only the
first bell tower of the Nativity façade, dedicated
to Barnabas the Apostle, was completed
within Gaudí's lifetime. To skip the queue, buy
advance tickets online.

🕐 0900–1800 daily (Oct–Mar), –2000 (Apr–Sep),
–1400 (Dec 25&26, Jan 1&6) 💲 €14.80/12.30
🏠 c/Mallorca 401, Dreta de l'Eixample
🔗 www.sagradafamilia.cat
🔗 Guided tour (incl. entry): €19.30/17.30

*"The height of Gaudi's creativity and genius are
captured in this monumental masterpiece."*

– Frank Plant

10 **Els Encants Vells**
Map B, P.102

In keeping with the traditions of this long-established flea market – Barcelona's biggest – local design firm b720 adhered to the concept of a meandering open space. Rag-lovers can poke around Moroccan and gypsy stalls, which sell everything from flooring to coffin keys, venturing from pitch to pitch via a swirling walkway that connects the space. A giant canopy suspended by metal casings protects from glaring midday sun but not from pick-pockets – pay close attention to your belongings during a visit.

🕐 0900-2000 (M, W, F-Sa)
🏠 av. Meridiana 73, Fort Pienc
URL www.encantsbcn.com

"Els Encants Vells is one of the three important new architectural features in Glòríes."
– Borja Martínez, Lo Siento

Narrow streets, eclectic bodegas and the smell of sea salt in the air – the seaside enclave next to Barceloneta beach has retained its charm as an old fishermen's village. Sample seafood from the local auction sale prepared fresh each day, along with which authentic tapas are famous citywide. After a stroll in the streets, enjoy a plate or two, or sit with a beer on a seaside terrace or the *chiringuitos* (beach bars) scattered around the 1,100-metre sandy beach. A swim in the gorgeous water is also highly recommended during summer. The beach is equipped with shower and bathrooms.

"Have good rice at Kaiku (pza. del Mar, 1). Bodega l'Electricitat (Sant Carles, 15) is another must."

– Atipus

12 Parc Güell
Map C, P.102

When Antoni Gaudí took up this project in 1900, it was intended as a private "garden city" with roughly 60 sea-facing houses. A Greek theatre and a hypostyle marketplace were to be provided among naturalistic decoration, but only two houses were eventually built. Gaudí later occupied the show home (now Gaudí House Museum), and enterpriser Eusebi Güell moved into the preexisting Casa Larrard which is now a school. Buy tickets in advance and arrive on the dot as visits to the Monumental zone are limited to 400 tickets and timed for half an hour from the reservation time.

🕐 0800-2000 daily, -2130 (May-Oct), 0830-1800 (Oct-Mar) 💲 €8/5.60 🏠 c/Olot, la Salut
🔗 www.parkguell.cat
🖊 Museum: 1000-2000 daily (Apr-Sep), -1800 (Oct-Mar), €5.50/4.50

"At this location (av. Coll del Portell, 112) you will not find any tourists around."

– UnitedFakes

Cultural & Art Space

Art factories, multidisciplinary galleries and creative spaces

It is becoming increasingly harder to speak of disciplines or genres in Barcelona's cultural scene since the launch of its "Art Factories" programme. This initiative, run by the city and its Culture Institute, transforms disused spaces into new powerhouses of culture and knowledge to promote social involvement. The opening of independent galleries and art spaces fosters a healthy tendency towards artistic cross-disciplinarity, allowing a liberal platform for individual and unconventional expressions through dance and movement, theatre, circus, visual and sound arts. Independent galleries, private initiatives and bookshops also highlight Barcelona's creative spirit with comprehensive showcases programmes in many disciplines, from architecture to spatial design. For regular cultural activities, spend time at Art Factories, Fabra i Coats (#16) and Hangar (www.hangar.org), as well as other centres like MACBA (#13), CCCB (#21) and Art Santa Mònica (www.artssantamonica.cat). Local and international artists work revolves at Mitte (#18), N2 Galería (#15) or Mutuo (#19). On Mount Montjuïc, visit Fundació Joan Miró (#14), MNAC (#22), CaixaForum Barcelona (#24) and the beautiful Botanic Garden in one trip.

Bernat Fortet Unanue
Multimedia designer

I worked in the entertainment industry in the past, but more recently focus on apps that change people life's in an impactful and meaningful way.

Fundació Joan Miró P.036

Crajes
Artist duo

Carla and Jessica as one: Crajes. We have been working together since 2009. The best definition for our work so far is "girly grotesque."

Hey
Graphic design studio

We are a small studio based in Barcelona and mostly work on brand identity, illustration and editorial design, and with geometry, colour and direct typography.

MACBA P.034

N2 Galería P.037

GIF ME
Multimedia design studio

An interactive installation service, and investigation project led by Daniel Armengol Altayó. Our final goal is to set a creative stage for new interactive experiences.

Museu Marítim P.040

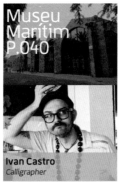

Ivan Castro
Calligrapher

Working freelance on calligraphy, lettering and typography and also teaching in Elisava, BAU and Visions. I am also a tropical bartending geek.

Christian Villacañas Camps, *Artist*

I usually spend the day drawing, reading comic books and graphic novels as well as writing. I'm also into learning about printing and bookbinding.

Fabra i Coats P.038

Mitte P.042

You are so Overrated
Art director & DJ

You are so Overrated is Chini. I'm a freelance art director, illustrator and DJ. You Are So Overrated is my personal project which includes illustrations, videos, comics and lots of other stuff!

Mutuo Centro de Arte
P.043

Miscelänea
P.044

Chamo San
Artist

I'm an illustrator born and based in Barcelona. I graduated in Fine Arts at Universitat de Barcelona and spent a year at École Nationale Supérieure des Beaux-Arts in París.

Dvein
Multimedia studio

A collaborative project by directors Fernando Domínguez, Teo Guillem and Carlos Pardo providing direction and art direction for live action and animation.

CCCB
P.045

Sergio Mora
Artist

I am an artist chameleon who lives in a spaceship landed on the artistic quarter of Poblenou. I am dedicated to painting, illustration, video, music, and performance.

MNAC
P.046

Museu Frederic Marès
P.048

Nacho Alegre
Publisher, apartamento

Born and raised in Barcelona, I work as a photographer and publisher (apartamento magazine) and live with my girlfriend and my dog.

Lusesita
Artist

My name is Laura, but I work under the name of Lusesita. I'm from Rioja and have lived in Barcelona for ten years where I work on sculpture and ceramics.

CaixaForum Barcelona
P.049

13 Museu d'Art Contemporani de Barcelona (MACBA)

Map E, P.107

Standing in marked contrast to its medieval locale, the white and unmistakably modern MACBA building is infused with late 20th century avant-garde attitude and El Raval's multicultural spirit. Every Saturday from 7pm live music and experimental art programmes take place next to its rolling exhibitions of contemporary art by Catalan and Spanish artists, North African and Eastern European art. The centre's substantial art book and catalogue archive is kept at MACBA Study Centre (*pl. dels Àngels 8, El Raval*), and is accessible with identification.

🕐 1100-1930 (M, W, Th-F), 1000-2100 (Sa), -1500 (Su & P.H.) 💲 €10/8
🏠 pl. dels Àngels 1, El Raval
📞 +34 93 41 20 810 🌐 www.macba.cat

"Awesome architecture and content. Enjoy one of the most popular skating spots (the square in front) in Europe, and nearby artistic and underground shops."

– Bernat Fortet Unanue

14 Fundació Joan Miró
Map G, P.109

Find the almost complete oeuvre of Joan Miró (1893–1983) on the slope of Montjuïc. Chiefly donated by Miró, over 14,000 pieces of abstract paintings, sculptures, textiles and ceramics reveal the itinerant artist's philosophies of art across the iconic building designed by Josep Lluís Sert (1902-83), Miró's lifelong friend. The museum also hosts a small contemporary art collection formed posthumously as a tribute. Expand the journey at Parc Joan Miró and Barcelona Airport Terminal B where more of his colossal pieces stand.

🕐 1000–1900 (Tu-Sa, Oct-Jun), –2000 (Tu-Sa, Jul-Sep), –2130 (Th), –1430 (Su & P.H.) 💲 €11/7
🏠 Parc de Montjuïc, Montjuïc 📞 +34 93 44 39 470
🔗 www.fundaciomiro-bcn.org

"It is a must see for Miró's lovers. And the building is wonderful."
– Hey

15 N2 Galería

Map D, P.104

Hiding away from Eixample's chaotic roads, the beautiful tree-lined Enric Granados street is graced with 20th-century architecture, broad walkways, outdoor cafés and reputable galleries. One of them is ground-floor gallery N2. Presenting eight exhibitions a year, mainly solo projects by young international artists, recent shows have presented Péjac, Crajes and Jorge Rodriguez Gerada, with installation, photography, video and fine art paintings. Enjoy art and the city on the street in equal amounts. Thursday evenings are chock-full with openings.

🕐 1100–1400, 1700–2030 (M–F) 🏠 c/Enric Granados, 61, L'Antiga Esquerra de l'Eixample
📞 +34 93 45 20 592 🔗 www.n2galeria.com
✏ Sa: by appointment only

"It's a great gallery for the variety of artists they present. Each exhibition is a surprise."

– Crajes

16 Fabra i Coats
Map A, P.102

An icon of Barcelona's industrial heritage, the red-brick spinning mill built in the 1920s now houses cultural incubator Fabra i Coats, one of the ten 'Art Factories' initiated by the city's Culture Institute. Since 2008, the 6,500sqm space has been shared among art units, micro-enterprises and emerging artists who periodically stage performances fusing theatre, dance, music and visual arts. In between, exhibitions, cultural festivals and movie premieres take place. Look out for little art projects scattered through the floors. Other well-loved "Factories" include Hangar (*Emilia Coranty 16, el Poblenou*).

🕐 0900–2230 (M–F), 1000–2100 (Sa)
🏠 c/Sant Adrià 20, Sant Andreu
📞 +34 93 25 66 150
🔗 fabraicoats.bcn.cat

"It's where I started my first project. Check the programme frequently as the activities change a lot from one day to another."

– GIF ME

17 Museu Marítim
Map E, P.107

With origins in the 14th century, this former royal shipyard, located at the waterfront of Ciutat Vella (Old Town district), now preserves Barcelona's naval history, with old maps, pictures, navigational instruments, test models and full size replica ships on permanent display. Boats of many different categories are represented, spanning medieval galleys, merchant ships, wooden submarine and racing boats dating back to the 1560s. The Gothic architecture, which will offer 10,000sqm of exhibition space after renovation, is due to fully reopen in late 2014. The project extends to Portal de Santa Madrona, the only remains of a medieval city old wall and gate at the fringe.

🕙 1000–2000 daily   💲 €5/4/2
🏠 av. de les Drassanes, el Raval
📞 +34 93 34 29 920
URL www.mmb.cat
🖉 Free admittance after 1500 (Su)

"The building itself is pretty impressive. Its permanent collection shows a lot of maritime culture and navigation history."
– Ivan Castro

18 **Mitte**
Map D, P.105

Equal parts art space, gallery and café, Mitte is a 300sqm site to get engrossed in art, books and conversations. Contemporary art and visual arts projects, installations and spontaneous creations by pre-eminent figures from Barcelona's art and design fields are regularly updated in a pop-up window, salon and wall, alongside live music shows, short film screenings and writing workshops. Exhibitions and openings here offer an ideal meeting point for new ideas, young talent and art enthusiasts.

🕙 1000-2200 (M-F)
🏠 c/Bailèn, 86, Dreta de l'Eixample
📞 +34 93 26 52 861
URL mitte-barcelona.com

"At the exhibition openings, beer is for free. Otherwise, it's always nice to have a coffee there."
– Christian Villacañas Camps

19 Mutuo Centro de Arte

Map E, P.107

A melting pot for Barcelona's vibrant art scene, this independent institution shows an amazing variety of artistic styles and voices. Independent producers, musicians and artists all appear in a weekly line-up, staged at the former garage, where the dim-lit, minimal interior is roughly divided between a mini-theatre, coffee lounge and art gallery and is accentuated with a mix of vintage leather chairs. Mutuo also sells designer goods ranging from jewellery, fashion, zines and art prints made by designers from around the world.

🕐 1100-1400 (W-F), 1700-2300 (W-Th),
1700-0100 (F-Sa), 1700-2300 (Su)
🏠 c/Julià Portet, 5, Bajos 1 y 2, el Gòtic
📞 +34 93 30 23 943 🔗 mutuocentro.com

"*The space and the exhibitions are some of the best in town.*"

– Chini aka You are so Overrated

20 Miscelänea
Map E, P.107

No better word than the name of this place could denote the assorted world of art enclosed in this artistic compound. With a gallery at the front and an "art laboratory" at the back, Miscelänea is a haven for things original and experimental shown in exhibitions, art markets, workshops and special events, curated in-house by a team of practising designers, illustrators and graphic artists. Creative brains set to work in the gallery's centre. They sell an interesting selection of independent publications, design objects and original prints selected from each show.

🕐 1700–2300 (W–Th, Su), –0200 (F–Sa)
🏠 c/Guardia 10, el Raval
☎ +34 93 31 79 398
URL www.miscelanea.info

"The gallery is a showcase of young talents and artworks. The upstairs is where their cozy beautiful bar hides."

– Chamo San

21 Centre de Cultura Contemporània de Barcelona (CCCB) *Map E, P.107*

With a solid multidisciplinary programme, CCCB connects visitors with the city and urban culture day in, day out. Diverse exhibitions, parties, outdoor cinema, music festivals and performances all alternately enliven the 19th century workhouse and courtyard, where cultural gatherings are completed with a nice bookshop and a cool nine-to-nine bar. Five-day literature festival Kosmopolis celebrates the oral, printed and digital art of words with exhibitions, talks and songs.

🕐 1100-2000 (Tu–Su & P.H.)
🏠 Montalegre, 5, el Raval
📞 +34 93 30 64 100
🌐 www.cccb.org

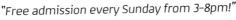

"*Free admission every Sunday from 3–8pm!*"
– Dvein

22 **Museu Nacional d'Art de Catalunya (MNAC)**
Map G, P.109

Admire one of world's most extensive Romanesque art collections inside the grand National Palace, built for the 1929 International Exposition. Comprising murals, wood carvings, metalwork and stone sculptures in diverse styles, the collection forms a valuable mark of Catalan visual art movements, which extends to Gothic, Renaissance, Baroque and Modern art. Exhibits also include a rotating selection of 19th to 20th century photography, design and drawings by important Spanish artists like Marià Fortuny, Antoni Gaudí and Salvador Dalí. Still thirst for more? MNAC organises guided tours to its art reserves on Fridays at 4.30pm, and architecture reserve on Sundays at 11am. Booking required.

🕐 1000–1800 (Tu–Sa, –2000 May–Sep), –1500 (Su & P.H.) 💲 €12/8.40
🏠 Palau Nacional, Montjuïc
📞 +34 93 62 20 360 🌐 www.mnac.cat

"If you want to relax a little, I recommend sitting on the stairs in front of MNAC and view Barcelona from Montjuïc."

– Sergio Mora

23 Museu Frederic Marès
Map E, P.107

Trained as a sculptor, notable for his post-civil war restoration work and monumental sculptures at Plaça de Catalunya, Frederic Marès (1893–1991) had also developed a love for collecting by the age of 18. Go straight up to the Collector's Cabinet to find thousands of 19th century objects, including clocks, pipes, weapons, cigar papers and toys that Marès used to stock in his study and donated to the city in 1944. The sculptor's own work and a sculpture collection are also exhibited in the medieval palace building, with a beautiful courtyard sitting next to Barcelona Cathedral.

🕐 1000–1900 (Tu–Sa), 1100–2000 (Su & P.H.)
💲 €4.20/2.40 🏠 pl. de Sant Iu 5–6, el Gòtic
📞 +34 93 25 63 500
🔗 www.museumares.bcn.cat

"It's a beautiful collector's museum that even locals haven't heard of."

– Nacho Alegre, apartamento

24 CaixaForum Barcelona
Map G, P.109

Lovers of Art Nouveau architecture and contemporary art will enjoy CaixaForum's changing shows held at this former textile factory, built in 1911 by legendary architect and a contemporary of Gaudí and Domènech i Montaner, Josep Puig i Cadafalch (1867–1956). To enter its superior exhibition space, visitors first encounter a minimalist "secret garden" before descending an escalator under a steel and glass tree sculpture to an open white stone courtyard, which were all added by Japanese architect Arata Isozaki (b. 1931) between 1999–2002. Book junkies should not miss the forum's media library and Laie bookshop, which stocks an excellent array of novels as well as books on architecture, art and film.

🕐 1000–2000 daily & P.H.
🏠 av. Francesc Ferrer i Guàrdia 6–8, la Font de la Guatlla 📞 +34 93 47 68 600
🔗 www.fundacio.lacaixa.es

"There are always interesting exhibitions alongside architecturally beautiful buildings."

– Lusesita

Markets & Shops

Handicrafts, design books and Catalan treats

Forget souvenirs on Ramblas. Instead, lose yourself in Catalan's designer shops, antique bazaars and centuries-old family businesses, many of whom are dedicated to producing original works. Friendly owners are happy to explain their selections or suggest products for your liking. Traditional groceries and food markets always guarantee a treasure hunt. If you're into handicrafts, Après Ski-Iriarte Iriarte (#31) and the annual festival Festivalet (www.festivalet.org) by Duduà (www.duduadudua. com) display handmade goods and accessories. Pay a visit to the designer-run Vostok Printing Shop (#30) too, for terrific silkscreen supplies, and El Ingenio (#27) for close-up views of Festes de la Mercé's gigantic heads. Those hungry for books, especially on art and design, should stop by La Central (www.lacentral.com) and Loring Art (www.loring-art.com), or Fatbottom (#32) for comics and art prints, while those hungry for delicious delicacies can satisfy cravings at Colmado Quílez (#35) or la Bouqería (#36). Vila Viniteca (www.vilaviniteca.es) sells exceptional Catalan wines, with the best coming from Priorat or Montsant region. Take that, a blanket, a few candles and head down to Nova Icària or Bogatell beach to set yourself up a nice picnic dinner by the sea.

Cristobal Castilla
Director, Aer Studio

I'm a co-founder of Aer Studio, specialising in digital design for web and mobile services. I love food (specially brunch) and am a table–tennis addict.

La Basílica Galería P.055

Georgina Santiago
Fashion designer

Born and based in Barcelona. I studied fashion design and worked as a forecaster. My aim is to become a trend forecaster, be inspired and inspire others.

Bruno Sellés
Creative director, Vasava

Born in Barcelona, I am the founder of design studio Vasava, which develops solutions ranging from typography, illustration, interactive design to animation.

Chandal P.054

El Ingenio P.056

Lyona
Filmmaker & illustrator

I started directing music videos for national and international bands after studying at ESCAC. I've published a children's book called "Yo mataré monstruos por ti" that is in its 7th edition.

Jazz Messengers P.058

Slow
Graphic design studio

We are an independent creative team whose work goes from conceptualisation to execution, emphasising on the process and exploring the limits of each idea.

Oriol Malet
Founder, Malet & Co.

I am an illustrator and work with La Vanguardia newspaper, TimeoutBCN entertainment magazine, the cultural magazine Jot Down, etc and illustrated books of all kinds.

SHObcn P.057

Vostok Printing Shop P.059

Miju Lee
Illustrator

South Korean now settled in Barcelona. I draw, paint and make things with clay. It's a great pleasure for me to connect with people with what I'm doing and sharing my view of the world.

Après Ski-Iriarte Iriarte
P.060

Fatbottom
P.061

Antonio Ladrillo
Graphic designer

My interests span abstract painting to philosophy, graffiti to publication. My design and illustrated works are a reflection of all these things.

P·A·R
Graphic design studio

A graphic design and art direction studio based in Barcelona by Iris Tarraga and Lucía Castro.

Kowasa
P.062

Laura Banchik
Fashion designer

I'm from Argentina and have lived in Barcelona since 2008. I design textiles and jewellery under the name of FARÖ. For me, Barcelona is a very inspiring place to live.

Vinçon
P.064

Colmado Quílez
P.066

David Espluga
Founder, espluga+associates

Creative director at espluga+associates. I love swimming, riding my bike and running. Love discovering new places to enjoy with people I love.

Dorian
Graphic design studio

Founded in 2009 by Gaëlle Alemany and Gabriel Morales, Dorian is a small studio located in Barcelona specialising in corporate identity, packaging and editorial design.

Mercat de la Boqueria
P.067

25 Chandal

Map E, P.107

Retro camera lovers and collectors will lose heart and mind to this captivating store. Stocking an unbeatable concentration of toy cameras, vintage cameras, rare models and accessories and film for Polaroid and lomography, Chandal also offers a Super 8 film package that covers film development. (Normally the service takes three to four weeks.) Music is another strength. Unconventional offerings, mainly vinyls, highlight dynamic selections in electronic, experimental and pop. If you are in luck, you'll uncover exhibitions or artist meetings during your visit.

🕐 1100–2100 (M–Sa)
🏠 c/Valldonzella 29, el Raval
📞 +34 93 30 28 471
URL shop.chandal.tv

"It also offers a great selection of vintage objects. Worth a visit when you are around the streets of CCCB (#21) and MACBA (#13)."

– Cristobal Castilla, Aer Studio

26 La Basílica Galería
Map E, P.107

If the labyrinthine streets of the Gothic Quarter have led you to carrer del Bisbe with a neogothic-style bridge built by architect Joan Rubió (1870-1952), walk a little further to carrer de Sant Sever and you'll find La Basílica Galería. Outlandish designs from about 200 jewel designers flank the stone-built premise in antique cabinets, emitting a curious fascination with nature and life. Polish artist and founder Piotr Rybaczek also lays out his striking goddess sculptures, dressed in rose petals and leaves. Across the alley is La Basílica Perfumery, offering sweet-smelling crafted perfume.

🕐 1100-1500, 1630-2030 daily
🏠 c/Sant Sever 7, el Gòtic
📞 +34 93 30 42 047
URL www.labasilicagaleria.com

"An impressive collection of contemporary jewellery and other pieces of art."

– Georgina Santiago

27 El Ingenio
Map E, P.107

With Salvador Dalí and Cirque du Soleil on their prestigious client list, El Ingenio has long been impressing people with its traditional carnival masks and costumes, and has been operating since 1838. Currently at the helm of the enterprise, Agustin Sevillano painstakingly handpaints oversize papier-mâché heads (*capgrossos*), bringing back to life as giants late legends like Pablo Picasso and Charlie Chaplin. The half-hidden, centuries-old shop also sells a dazzling range of magic gadgets, puppets, juggling stuff and nostalgic handmade old-school toys. Fascinating.

🕐 1000-1330, 1615-2000 (M-F),
1100-1400, 1700-2030 (Sa)
🏠 c/Rauric 6, el Gòtic
📞 +34 93 31 77 138
URL www.elingeniodelsmalabars.com

"Never judge a shop by it's website. In an alternative reality, this would be Willy Wonka's games room."

– Bruno Sellés, Vasava

28 SHObcn

Map D, P.104

Opened in 2009, SHObcn continuously strives to push the benchmark for the international graphic art scene. Local and world-famous designers and artists have left their mark in this corner store; Badalona-based collective Barri Groc's handdrawn murals are eye-catching in the main room, Barcelona illustrator Cesc Grané's cartoonish aliens pop in the middle room and then a sticker-filled wall and racks of print tees, fanzines and art toys produced by the like of Kaws, Frank Kozik and Emilio Garcia follow. At the back is a versatile space that hosts exhibitions and launch parties.

🕐 1100-2030 (M-Sa)
🏠 trav. de Gràcia 163, Vila de Gràcia
📞 +34 64 72 76 877
URL shobcn.com

"Part art gallery, part design concept store and part creative studio, SHObcn delivers unique urban style to the heart of Gràcia."

– Lyona

29 Jazz Messengers
Map D, P.104

The name "Jazz Messengers" is a tribute to jazz giant Art Blakey and his hard-bop band and a note on the genre they specialised in. Over 15,000 records (CDs, LPs, and vinyl) and books present a comprehensive collection of international and Catalan labels, re-issues, hard-to-find albums and secondhand records showcasing gems in jazz classic, modern jazz, West Coast and Latin jazz, among others. Since 1980, the store has promised to supply "the best jazz at the best price." Their monthly catalogue details latest promotions and new arrivals to the store.

🕐 1030–1400, 1600–2030 (Tu–F), 1030–1430, 1630–2030 (Sa) 🏠 Córsega 202, Bajos-Derecha, L'Antiga Esquerra de l'Eixample
📞 +34 93 44 07 105 URL www.jazzmessengers.com

"For jazz lovers (like me)."
– Oriol Malet, Malet & Co.

The ultimate playground for designers and craft enthusiasts, Vostok is stuffed with all sorts of first-class art supplies needed for silk screening, block printing, lettering and lithography. Inks, cutting tools, stencils and stamps are systematically categorised, alongside printing kits for various skill levels and materials for batik. If you are unsure what you need or how to transfer your thoughts into your prints, take advantage of the specialist staff. Practicing designer Alexis Rom occasionally runs workshops to demonstrate basic and unconventional stamping and engraving skills.

🕐 1000–1400, 1600–2000 (M–F),
1100–1430 (Sa) 🏠 c/Portal Nou 31,
Sant Pere, Santa Caterina i la Ribera
📞 +34 93 31 91 889
URL www.vostokshop.eu

"Go open-minded and let them tell you about new products."

– Slow

31 Après Ski-Iriarte Iriarte
Map F, P.108

Jewellery designer Lucía Vergara started Après Ski in 2009 after working at Spanish brands Lydia Delgado and Ailanto. Since then, she has been creating unique pieces that identify with vintage aesthetics, using golden brass and resin pieces, ceramic beads, wood or antique fabrics to illustrate nature and the universe. Don't shy away from talking to Vergara, who shares her showroom and studio space with friend and fashion designer Carolina Iriarte of Iriarte Iriarte, a quality leather goods brand.

🕐 1000-1400, 1600-2000 (M-Sa)
🏠 c/Cotoners 12, Sant Pere, Santa Caterina i la Ribera
URL www.apresskishop.com, www.iriarteiriarte.com

"If you are looking for some authentic Spanish design, I strongly recommend you to visit Après Ski's shop and look at her collection."
– Miju Lee

32 Fatbottom
Map E, P.107

Fatbottom has a nose for good fanzines and underground comics. Stocking an eclectic range of classics, including everything from comic strip collections and translated works to some of the weirdest sci-fi, sex comics and children's books published around the world, this young bookshop is a repertory of contemporary graphic novels for every taste and age. Besides illustrated books, also expect to discover music, art prints, posters and stationery not seen in mainstream outlets. Fatbottom even hosts small live concerts on occasions.

🕐 1700-2100 (M-F), 1100-1400, 1800-2100 (Sa)
🏠 c/Lluna 10, el Raval   ☎ +34 93 17 98 957
🌐 fatbottombooks.com

"Try attend an opening of one of their shows. They have a very good selection and you can feel the passion for this kind of publications on the air."

– Antonio Ladrillo

33 Kowasa

Map D, P.104

Entirely dedicated to the world of image, Kowasa has a good store of magazines, monographs, retrospects, out-of-prints, catalogues, yearbooks, portfolios and handbooks, in different languages – all with a strong focus on photography or visual culture. Take a few hours to rummage their shelves. Among the 11,000 titles amassed during the store's 15 years in existence, there are bound to be a few rare gems awaiting discovery. The floor above the retail space is Kowasa Gallery, which rotates Spanish and foreign photography exhibits.

 ⏱ 1000–2030 (M-F), 1000–1500, 1600–2030 (Sa) 🏠 c/Mallorca 235, Dreta de l'Eixample 📞 +34 93 21 58 058 🔗 www.kowasa.com ⊘ Gallery: 1630–2030 (Tu-Sa)

"If you are peckish when you leave the shop, you can always trust Cornelia&Co (c/València 225) or Crustó (c/València 246)."
– P·A·R

34 Vinçon
Map D, P.104

Lodged in the former home of painter Ramón Casas (1866-1932) which was designed by architect Antoni Rovira i Rabassa (1845-1919) in 1899, Vinçon is a temple of clever, contemporary homeware and furnishing design. While the architecture and its select inventory fever imagination of an über-cool living space, regular collaborations between the shop and international artists vouch for an inspiring experience that starts from window displays and ventures all the way through to its paper bags. Do not miss La Sala Vinçon, the ground-floor gallery oriented toward industrial and graphic design. Upstairs find past bag designs by the best Catalan designers and a close side view of Gaudí's La Pedrera.

🕐 1000-2030 (M-F), 1030-2100(Sa)
🏠 pg. de Gràcia, 96, Dreta de l'Eixample   📞 +34 93 21 56 050
URL www.vincon.com

"It's simply an amazing store with lots of things to love."
– Laura Banchik aka FARÖ

35 Colmado Quílez
Map D, P.104

With floor-to-ceiling shelves chock-full of gourmet foods including liquors and wines, cured Ibérico hams, sausages, cheeses, teas, confectionary and preserves, this grocer's history shares its beginnings with the Palau de la Música Catalana, and began trading in 1908. Over 10,000 products are stocked, with a team of knowledgeable señores in blue smocks waiting to help you buy from your list. The LaFuente family, who owns the store and is known for its wineries, also sells their own cava Spanish sparkling wine and lines of products, from tinned foods to foie gras.

🕐 0900-1400, 1630-2030 (M-Sa)
🏠 rbla. Catalunya 63, Dreta de l'Eixample 📞 +34 93 21 58 785
🌐 www.lafuente.es

"Here you can buy the items for the most premium picnic ever."

– David Espluga, espluga+associates

36 Mercat de la Boquería
Map E, P.107

Any traveller should visit la Boquería at least once to discover Catalunya's passion for food. Its privileged location, together with gourmet offerings as varied as chocolate to fowl, seafood to innards, and amazing personalities at over 200 stalls and eateries prompt locals and tourists to wake up at the early hours to explore and enjoy the food. Among the many creatives who recommended la Boquería, one-third highlighted Bar Pinotxo for tapas. Go for jamón, cheese, olive oil and fruits here. Individual stores might close at 4pm from Monday to Thursday.

🕗 0800–2030 (M–Sa)
🏠 Rambla, 91, el Raval
☎ +34 93 31 82 584
URL www.boqueria.info

"The stands and bars closer to 'Las Ramblas' are more touristy and expensive than those near the back entrance."
– Dorian

Restaurants & Cafés

Gourmet tapas, seafood specialties and homemade vermouth

Barcelona has developed its age-old gastronomic theories alongside influences from Andalusian and Galician cuisine, and benefits from fresh local greens and fruits. Its coastal location adds an exquisite variety of fresh fish and shellfish, to inspire specialties like paella that are typically good in Barceloneta, the old fisherman quarter. Add to this good bread, cured sausages, calçots (scallion, plentiful in spring) and Catalan wine for a hint of the mouthwatering dishes on offer. Try the notable Tickets (*www.ticketsbar.es*) and Cal Pep (*www.calpep.com*) or, for a more casual dining, Bodega La Palma (#46) or Bodega l'Electricitat (*c/Sant Carles 15, La Barceloneta*). La Pubilla (#38), little bars at el Mercat del Ninot (*www.mercatdelninot.com*) and la Boquería (#36) are also clever choices for tasty homemade food and real deal tapas. For innovative fare, check out pop-up restaurant La Santa (voluntad) (#42) and Fàbrica Moritz (#47), and on a Sunday morning follow the trend and quaff vermouth at Morro Fi (#52) and small nibbles before lunch at 2pm.

Bea Bascuñán
Graphic designer

I am in charge of Valencia-based studio Espacio Paco Bascuñán (EPB) and founder of independent publishing label, Publications for Pleasure. I also run a small screenprinting atelier.

La Pubilla
P.073

Jordi Rins
Graphic designer

I'm currently working freelance with film production companies. I like designing film posters and promotional materials for movies.

Pablo Rovalo
Director, Research Studios

Trained as a visual designer in Mexico City and London, I live in Barcelona as a media professional with experience ranges from environmental graphics to motion graphics.

Granja
Petitbo
P.072

El Equipo Creativo
Interior design duo

Oliver Franz Schmidt and Natali Canas del Pozo began collaboration in 2010. The duo specialises in designing gastronomic spaces as well as brand and commercial projects.

La Cantina
de Palo Alto
P.077

Petz Scholtus
Founder, yök Casa + Cultura

I'm a no-stuff–designer, eco-creative and future hotelier from Luxembourg. My goal is to create a business for People, Planet and Profit that embraces the local culture in a fun and elegant way.

Bar
Velódromo
P.074

**Marc Castellví
Hernandez**, *Filmmaker*

Born in Barcelona in 1989. I'm currently working freelance. I'm also involved in No más – de mamá, a gastronomic, graphic and audiovisual project.

Ikibana
P.076

La Santa
(voluntad)
P.078

Sergi Puyol
Illustrator

I've published three comic books with Apa-Apa Còmics and run the Colibrí Fanzine with Toni Mascaró from Apa-Apa. I'm also a drummer and composer for my bands.

La
Milagrossa
Milanesa
P.079

Cuines Santa
Caterina
P.080

Reskate Studio
Design studio

We are María López and Javier de Riba who create with sustainability in mind. Our work touches on graphic design, illustration, photography, video and installations.

Lucía Vergara Ballester
Jewellery designer, Après Ski

I love what I do, and so I spend most of my time in the studio hand-lacquering and sanding pieces, while listening to music planning my next holiday/trip.

Dolç i Salat
P.082

Mark Brooks
Graphic designer

I'm born here to a Catalan mother and an American father. I'm trained and worked as a designer in New York until 2010, and founded Mark Brooks Graphik Design in Barcelona.

Bodega
La Palma
P.083

Fàbrica
Moritz
P.084

Tabula Rasa Studio
Graphic design studio

A young studio from Barcelona with graphic design base and experience in UX and UI. We develop projects ranging from corporate identity to web or apps design.

Laia Clos
Founder, Mot

I started my studio Mot in 2006 and now also teach at the Eina University (UAB). I am the vice president of the ADG FAD (Art Directors and Graphic Designers Association).

Can Maño
P.085

37 Granja Petitbo
Map D, P.105

Large windows, high ceilings and sweet decorations made from all sorts of bits and bobs help make this charming corner café a local hot spot for weekend brunch and peaceful off-peak haven despite its location at the very centre of Eixample. Fresh ingredients and precision cooking create unforgettable flavours in well-presented simple dishes like crunchy green salads, quinoa risotto, brie and smoked salmon on toast topped with poached eggs, and white chocolate pancakes. Granja Petitbo is vegetarian-friendly and serves real coffee at all hours.

🕑 *0830-2200 (M-W), -0000 (Th), -0100 (F), 1000-0100 (Sa), 1000-1700 (Su)*
🏠 *pg. Sant Joan 82, Dreta de l'Eixample*
📞 *+34 93 26 56 503* 📘 *Granja Petitbo*

"Best to go during the week as the weekend and especially brunch time gets quite busy. Juices and cheesecake are highly recommended!"

– Bea Bascuñán, Espacio Paco Bascuñán

38 La Pubilla
Map D, P.104

It is no surprise to find local cuisine at La Pubilla, as young owner and chef Alexis Peñalve draws his inspirations from Mercat de la Llibertat (Freedom Square), the farmers' market opposite. The trusty *menú del dia* at this neighbourhood cafe features tempting appetisers like pickled mushroom salad, cream of chickpea soup with olive sausage or mussels, followed by meat or seafood dishes and desserts for just €14. Every table receives complimentary bread and olives and a glass of wine, and vegetarian dishes can often be arranged on request.

🕐 0830-1700 (M), -0000 (Tu-Sa)
📍 pl. de la Llibertat 23, Vila de Gràcia 📞 +34 93 21 82 994
f La Pubilla Gràcia

"This is where the best traditional and modern food of Barcelona can be found at a good price."

– Jordi Rins

39 Bar Velódromo
Map D, P.104

Come here for the splendor of the art deco building at the upper end of carrer Muntaner and then stay for a palatable breakfast or choice of tapas. A popular meeting spot for politicians and artists in the mid-1900s, and later a nightclub, the establishment gained new life as a trendy cafe under the reins of Jordi Vilà, owner of Michelin-starred Alkimia (*c/ Indústria 79, Vila de Gràcia*). Make your way up the original staircase to the mezzanine floor to watch life downstairs. Standout dishes include *huevos estrellados* (fried eggs). The endearing menu design updates once a month.

🕐 *0600-0200 daily*
🏠 *c/Muntaner 213, L'Antiga Esquerra de l'Eixample*
📞 *+34 93 43 06 022*

"Great retake on a classic Barcelona Bar."
– Pablo Rovalo, Research Studios

40 Ikibana
Map E, P.106

From food philosophy to dazzling interior, Ikibana is a bright fusion of Japanese and Brazilian cultures. Cocktail bar, open kitchen and tables divide the place into several islands, and diners can watch mixologists shake drinks and chefs ornament plates with premium fish and tropical ingredients. Finish your gastronomic journey with a Sake Mojito, or "Cerveza," Ikibana's award-winning sweet course. Or dare yourself to try wasabi ice-cream.

🕐 1300-0100 (M-F), -0300 (Sa-Su)
🏠 av. del Paral-lel, 148, Sant Antoni
📞 +34 93 42 44 648
URL www.ikibanagastroclub.es

"*A cool place for dinner and cocktails in Paralelo avenue, the theatre avenue in Barcelona.*"

– El Equipo Creativo

41 La Cantina de Palo Alto
Map J, P.110

Less than ten minutes walk away from Metro station Selva de Mar (L4) stands Javier Mariscal's plant-covered fortress, Palo Alto. Buried among the lush mixed vegetation are the offices of some 20 creative units, outdoor meeting rooms, a kitchen garden and a staff bar that welcomes the public during office hours. La Cantina is a popular lunch place amongst creatives where Mediterranean cuisine is prepared with locally-sourced ingredients. Mariscal is also the creator of 1992 Barcelona Olympics' mascot, Cobi, and Oscar-nominated animated film *Chico & Rita* (2010).

🏠 c/Pellaires, 30-38, Diagonal Mar i el Front Marítim del Poblenou
📞 +34 93 30 70 974
f La Cantina de Palo Alto

"Friday is paella day and if you're lucky you might spot Javier Mariscal himself!"

– Petz Scholtus, yök Casa + Cultura

42 La Santa (voluntad)

Map E, P.107

The first edition of La Santa (voluntad) was a month long pop-up project. With the aim of publishing a cookbook, the pioneers behind local food blog No más – de mamá invited the city's foodies to a homely roof terrace in Raval in spring 2013 for modern imaginative Mediterranean cuisine. Now the project welcomes four guests each sitting to sample new multi-course menus, with the project's founders joining during the dessert course for a chat and feedback. The initiative was created by a trio of good friends – chef Carlos Román, and designers Marc Castellví and Adrià Pifarre. Subscribe to their newsfeed for future events.

🕐 1400-1600, flexible days
🏠 c/Picalquers 3, àtic 3, el Raval
URL www.lasantavoluntad.com,
www.nomasdemama.com

"Best of all is that the price is what you think the meal was worth! If you'd like to come to La Santa, ask at bendigo@lasantavoluntad.com."

– Marc Castellví Hernandez, No más – de mamá

43 La Milagrossa Milanesa
Map C, P.103

Despite the superb lineup of independent bands, the weekend music shows don't outshine the delicious Argentinian specialities at this charming little bar. Among walls plastered with vintage posters and patterned tiles, medium-sized plates of crusty *empanadas* (meat-stuffed pies), *milanesa* (breaded cutlet), *entraña* (diced skirt steak with bread) and cured cheeses, among other options, can be sampled at prices as low as €4, which also covers beer, vermouth or wine. Weekend programmes start as early as 1pm. You Fucking' Hippies, a group born during Primavera Sound 2011, presents local independent music groups every Sunday from 8.30pm.

🕐 2000–0200 (Tu–Su)
🏠 c/Torrent de les Flors 94, Vila de Gràcia
f la.m.milanesa

"They have an amazing selection of live bands almost every week."

– Sergi Puyol

 Cuines Santa Caterina
Map F, P.108

A direct way to experience and gain inspiration from the fresh greens, fish and meat offered at Market Santa Caterina is to eat at their kitchen and tapas bar. Dishes like *botifarra*, grilled provolone cheese, Thai curry, tempura vegetables – are created using ingredients spotted under the colourful mosaicked canopy, cooked in Mediterranean, Asian or Spanish kitchens, and washed down with a good wine or freshly-pressed juices. Market Santa Caterina is a marketplace for all things grown in the area. One or two stalls are dedicated to Jabugo Ibérico ham.

🕐 1300-1600 (M-F), -1630 (Sa-Su), 2000-0000 (Su-W), -0030 (Th-Sa), Bar: 0900-2330 (Su-W), -0030 (Th-Sa) 🏠 av. Francesc Cambó, 16, Sant Pere, Santa Caterina i la Ribera 📞 +34 93 26 89 918 **URL** grupotragaluz.com/en/restaurante/cuines-caterina

"The bar is where you can ask for a quick but delicious tapas and the restaurant for seasonal dishes with market products that are cooked in sight."

– Reskate Studio

45 **Dolç i Salat**
Map F, P.108

Dolç i Salat is a cosy intimate café behind Market Santa Caterina and perfect to nestle during a lazy morning or afternoon. Mixed antique furniture, handwritten menus and decoration are just as sweet as the toothsome pastries and cakes offered, and Roberta, the affable owner who plays music from her old record player. Apart from the "Dolç (sweet)," expect typical southern Italian "Salat (savoury)" items like mozzarella porchetta and pasticciotto. Dolç i Salat is affiliated to the famed trattoria Le Cucine Mandarosso (c/Verdaguer i Callís, 4, la Ribera) near the Palau de la Música.

🕐 0800–2100 (Tu-F), 0900–1400 (Sa)
🏠 c/Colomines 6, Sant Pere,
Santa Caterina i la Ribera 📞 +34 93 31 90 502
URL www.lecucinemandarosso.com

"It is where I have breakfast everyday. Go for the bagel with olives, avocado, and ricotta. All of her cakes are delicious."

– Lucía Vergara Ballester, Après Ski

46 Bodega La Palma
Map E, P.107

Hidden in one of the historic Gothic Quarter's narrow streets, this wine house boasts more than 75 years of history, but remains young at heart. Try a true Catalan meal or authentic tapas (especially omelettes) served by warm, friendly staff in this unfussy traditional bodega (wine cellar) setting. The barman has encyclo-pedia-like knowledge on whiskies and other spirits. Let yourself be advised. Raw artisanal cheeses are some of the best you'll taste.

🕓 0900–0000 (M-F), 1200– (Sa)
🏠 c/Palma de Sant Just 7, el Gòtic
📞 +34 93 31 50 656

"Best if you go on a week day. Take the L4 (yellow) subway to Jaume I and beware of the pickpockets."
– Mark Brooks, Mark Brooks Graphik Design

47 Fàbrica Moritz
Map E, P.107

Fàbrica Moritz, the first beer factory in Barcelona and benchmark of Catalan beer since 1856, is now a hip gastronomic destination where you can taste fresh, unpasteurized beer poured straight from the barrels at the microbrewery. Masterfully revived by starchitect Jean Nouvel, the 19th century building is separated into five zones, where you can revel in finger-licking tapas or brunch next to a vertical garden, buy signature Nouvel-designed Moritz chairs or partake in varying events held in underground fermentation halls. Go with time to spare if you plan on trying the factory route.

🕐 0600-0300 daily
🏠 rda. Sant Antoni 39, Sant Antoni
📞 +34 93 42 60 050
URL www.moritz.com

"There are interesting events every week. Check their facebook page and you'll surely find something to raise your interest."

– Tabula Rasa Studio

48 Can Maño
Map H, P.110

Everything from the hexagonal tiles and framed yellowed reviews, to the ceiling fans and handwritten bills, as well as the lovable father-owner informs this little tavern's long history of homestyle cooking. Fish, prawn (*gamba*) and squid fried or grilled with garlic and parsley continues to win over locals in the old fishermen's quarter, with tables highly sought even in the hottest months. Can Maño is very small and serves dinner only during the week. Arrive early as queues form way before opening time at 8pm.

🕐 0800–2300 (M), 0830–1600 (Tu–Sa),
2000–2300 (Tu–F)
🏠 c/Baluard 12, La Barceloneta
📞 +34 93 31 93 082

"*Normally filled by locals, it's a very good place to taste fresh and grilled seafood at very good prices. A really authentic and vivid place.*"

– Laia Clos, Mot

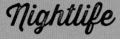

Nightlife

Live bands, cocktail classics and thematic concerts

Wherever you go at night in Barcelona, good music follows you around. Get sweaty dancing to DJ-spun disco and pop, and then wallow in an eclectic mix of jazz, roots, reggae, soul, techno, flamenco, caplo, funk or fusion at Heliogàbal (#56) or head to Sala Apolo (#57) for live shows and musician-run taprooms like Vinilo (#50) for more select playlists. Hit things off on a high note -- pick a high ground and view Barcelona's spectacular sunset, be it at Tibidabo, Bunker del Carmel (#4), or Mount Montjuïc. Arrive around 7.30pm in summer or 3.30pm in winter to watch the city fade into the dusky pink light. After, sip cocktails that carry a taste of the 1950s at Boadas Cocktails (#53), watch a play in a 135 year-old location (#54), feel the energy of traditional Spanish Copla tunes at O'Barquiño (#59), or hit any of the terraces in Gràcia (if you're into beer, give Voll-Damm a shot). Summer travellers should hit up the great indie and electronic bands that appear at Primavera Sound (*www.primaverasound.com, May/June*) and Piknic Electronik (*piknicelectronik.es, June through to September*).

Amaia Arrazola
Artist

Born in Basque, I studied advertising in Madrid and work in Barcelona. I like everything that has to do with illustration.

Vinilo
P.091

Paula Bonet
Artist

Based in Barcelona since 2012, I paint and draw for magazines, editorials, private commissions and also do mural paintings.

Pau Alekumsalaam
Graphic designer

Professional whistler and loser of valuable objects, student of all, almost guitarist for a day, writer without orthographic manual, compulsive winner and eternal aspirant to intellectual.

Cal Brut
P.090

La Cervecita
P.092

Querida
Graphic design studio

We are a design and communication studio based in Barcelona.

Boadas
Cocktails
P.094

Óscar Germade
Creative director, Solo

Creative director of an independent graphic design studio in Barcelona working on identity, editorial and packaging design.

Pietari Posti
Founder, Studio Posti

I'm a Finnish illustrator and graphic designer enjoying life in Barcelona. I get a kick from everything visual, from Belgium comics to modern furniture design.

Morro Fi
P.093

Bar de l'Antic
Teatre
P.095

clase bcn
Graphic design studio

A Barcelona-based studio made up of ten young multidisci-plinary professionals who work on all areas of design, but pay particular attention to typeface and the element of surprise.

Ocaña
P.096

Heliogàbal
P.097

BET
Fashion design studio

Barcelona Experimentació Tèxtil (BET) is a project created by three designers in Barcelona driven by the need to experi-ence the many lives and pos-sibilities of textile language.

Physalia
Multimedia design studio

Founded in 2007 in Barcelona, we work on 3D animation, photography, live action, stop-motion, robotics, electronics, etc. To us, every new project is a unique work of craftsman-ship.

Sala Apolo
P.098

David Melgarejo Vicente
Journalist

I am a journalist and art and fashion creative. Urban culture and video art are two of my biggest obsessions. Open your eyes because there are a lot of interesting stories surrounding you. You just have to find it!!

Cèntric
Canalla
P.099

O'Barquiño
P.100

Cristina Spanò
Illustrator

I work primarily on editorial and comics, and projects with the collective Teiera. I look for ironic and direct ideas in my work.

Soledad Arismendi
Web designer

I'm director of "This is not a Company," with a passion for beauty in all its glory. My love for modern technologies has assisted me in setting up a plat-form for artists: WeArt Festival.

JazzSí Club
P.101

49 Cal Brut
Map F, P.108

A reggae bar with true reggae soul. Called "Dirty House," this hangout is brimming with retro posters, Minorcan gin bottles, absurd signs, characterful knick-knacks and Caribbean music. Bob Marley overlooks a kitchenette, where the barmen flip dishes as well as glasses to prepare hearty tapa dishes made to match drink of the moment, homemade vermouth. Naturally, Cal Brut also carries Minorcan gin and a selection of Spanish and imported beers (from Jamaica, Belgium, Czech, the Netherlands, Germany).

🕐 1900-0100 daily 🏠 c/Princesa, 42, Sant Pere, Santa Caterina i la Ribera 🔗 www.calbrut.cat

"Not many bars in Born have barmen who can remember you and your drink after your first visit. A very, very friendly place to spend the night."

– Amaia Arrazola

No attempt is made to create a bohemian night spot. Owner and guitarist with local band Inspira, Jordi Lanuza's carefully crafted playlist comprises such variation as classic rock, trip hop, jazz and twee pop, that turns this bar into an intimate spot dedicated to vinyl. Beside crowds of friendly locals, great musicians of the Catalan music scene are often seen holding a beer at the bar. Plaça de la Vila, the mythical neighbourhood square, is just around the corner, an added bonus.

🕐 2000–0230 daily 🏠 c/Matilde 2, Vila de Gràcia
URL myspace.com/barvinilo f vinil0 bar

"*Good music, nice people and great location. The owner, Jordi Lanuza is a really friendly guy that will receive you with a big smile.*"
– Paula Bonet

51 La Cervecita
Map I, P.110

Both an emporium and tasting room, La Cervecita is a beer-lover's paradise where over 200 obscure craft beers and imports can be sampled and purchased. American Flying Dog (porter), Scottish Brewdog (imperial stout) and Catalan lagers, are among selections that won over the hearts of owners Angie Gesteira and Joaquín Jané, but they can be fickle – the selection, served by the bottle with some on tap, constantly evolves and expands. At times, the couple also produces their own specialty brews for celebrations, such as the shop's November anniversary.

⏱ *1700–2130 (M), 1130–1400 (Tu-F),*
1700–2130 (Tu-W), –2030 (Th), –2230 (F-Sa)
🏠 *C/Llull 184, el Poblenou* ☎ *+34 93 48 69 271*
f *La Cervecita nuestra de cada día*

"It's like home to rest. Come in a lazy evening on a weekday and enjoy the calm of the local people. They have over 100 varieties of beers, and cheap! Halleluja!"

– Pau Alekumsalaam

 52 Morro Fi
Map E, P.106

From food blog to bar, Morro Fi seems to know well what can make life better. To get a good idea, ask for Marcel's "*vermut preparat,*" Morro Fi's housemade vermouth (in Morro Fi-designed bottles, no less). The drink is recommended alongside extra thick crisps and other typical faves – canned mussels, cured anchovy fillets and crunchy green olives considered more "*aperitiu* (appetisers)" than tapas. Although a popular place for a drink after-hours, the hipster ritual in Barcelona is to sip vermouth just before Sunday lunch. To get in on the trend, make sure your Saturday night doesn't blot your Sunday morning.

🕐 1800–2300 (M–Th), 1200–1600, 1800–2300 (F–Sa), 1200–1600 (Su & P.H.) 🏠 c/Consell de Cent 171, la Nova Esquerra de l'Eixample 🔗 morrofi.cat

"Another 'best' vermouth place with the best spicy chips, best vermouth, best beer, best people, and best waiter in town."
– Querida

53 **Boadas Cocktails**
Map E, P.107

Framed reportage prints, wooden stools and, more importantly, champion cocktails – good old tradition is well-kept in this mahogany-filled bar. Possibly the oldest barroom in town, opened by Havana-inspired mixologist Miguel Boadas in 1933, Boadas shakes a dry martini famous citywide and daiquiris that have lured esteemed clients like poet Sagarra and Nobel-prize winning playwright Jacinto Benavente. Joan Miró even has a concoction dedicated to him. The bar hasn't rested on its laurels – if you're up for something new, let the sleek-headed professionals on staff surprise you.

🕐 1200–0200 (M–Th), –0300 (F–Su)
🏠 c/Tallers 1, Vallvidrera, el Tibidabo i les Planes
📞 +34 93 31 89 592 **URL** boadascocktails.com

"Ask for an 'Old-Fashioned', nowhere is it better than in this place."

– Óscar Germade, Solo

54 Bar de l'Antic Teatre
Map E, P.107

Despite a central location, this little theatre can be hard to find. Don't let it fool you – it's not to be missed. Establishing itself as an independent space for contemporary performance art, Antic Teatre runs an eclectic programme, from circus to concerts and dance that deals with society, culture, politics and contemporary thought. The inner terrace and courtyard displays anarchic vegetation but is an oddly charming place where anyone can come anytime to slug back a beer. To enter, look for a small door in the middle of a dark alley south of Palau de la Música.

🕐 1000-2330 (M-Th), -0000 (F), 1600-0000 (Sa), -2330 (Su) 🏠 c/Verdaguer i Callís 12, Sant Pere, Santa Caterina i la Ribera
📞 +34 93 31 52 354 🌐 www.anticteatre.com

"*Escape the chaotic city to Antic Teatre's big courtyard terrace. At night it can get quite full and noisy but the drink prices are cheap.*"

– Pietari Posti, Studio Posti

55 Ocaña
Map E, P.107

With enticing outdoor terrace facing the beautiful Plaça Reial, a chic café, the intriguing Apotheke cocktail bar, and a high-ceilinged restaurant connected to a club, Ocaña understandably seduces. Designer chairs, vintage fixtures and original pillars with oak flooring harmoniously blend within this fabulous building, a restoration by Albert Guilleumas and Mireia Campa, which took eight years to complete. Chat over a chilled frothy beer or a fancy cocktail, sample modern Catalan cuisine, and then dance under the DJ's gaze till the wee hours.

🕐 1700-0230 (M-Th), -0300 (F), 1100-0300 (Sa),
-0230 (Su) 🏠 pl. Reial 13-15, el Gòtic
📞 +34 93 67 64 814 🔲 www.ocana.cat

"It's real fun with a mixed crowd. Take care in the surrounding area though."

– clase bcn

56 Heliogàbal
Map D, P.104

Besides being a teeny little bar, Heliogàbal is a multidisciplinary platform for emerging talent and an unmissable stop for indie bands touring Barcelona. Their cultural offering is diverse. Several nights a week you can enjoy poetry readings, experimental music and live jazz concerts followed by open jam sections in this compact space. Photography exhibitions, magazine launches, audiovisual screenings and much more also take place. As a well known spot in the neighbourhood it fills up quickly.

🕐 2130 till late (W–Su)
🏠 c/Ramón y Cajal 80, Vila de Gràcia 📞 +34 93 67 63 132
URL www.heliogabal.com
💲 Cash only

"Arrive a little before 9pm, opening time. Do not miss the atmosphere at the entrance in between concerts. Sometimes the best parts happen outside."

– BET

57 **Sala Apolo**
Map E, P.107

Cutting-edge gigs and wild parties are non-stop at this top-ranked concert hall and club. Visiting and homegrown bands occupy main venue Sala Apolo and annexe La [2] de Apolo in the early evening, with musical styles ranging from techno through to reggae and swing. Indie rock and pop leads the way on "Nasty Mondays". Refined-pop lovers should also look out for "Old Wave New Wave" hosted by Miqui Puig every month. At midnight, the music halls morph into crazy club houses. Dance hard into the small hours every night except Sunday.

🕐 💲 *Showtime & ticket price vary with programmes* 🏠 *c/Nou de la Rambla 113, el Poble-sec* 📞 *+34 93 44 14 001* 🆄🆁🅻 *www.sala-apolo.com*

"Get ready to party. The best DJ's coming on Fridays."
– Physalia

58 Cèntric Canalla
Map E, P.107

Friendly and convivial, Cèntric Canalla has a classy interior mostly inherited from original occupant, Cèntric Bar, which first opened in 1941. Local interior designer Pilar Libano has given it a fantastic facelift, turning the place into a chic, retro café-bar now best known for their gin and tonics. Offered are more than 30 gins for pairings of your choosing. The kitchen serves excellent grub too, from hearty tapas plates to larger selections like burgers and omelette, as well as homemade pies. Head to the room at the back if you want to sit and eat with a group of friends.

🕐 0800-0100 (M-Th), -0200 (F), 0900-0200 (Sa), -0100 (Su)
📍 c/Ramelleres 27, el Raval
🄵 Cèntric Canalla

"Gintonics!!"
– David Melgarejo Vicente

59 O'Barquiño
Map E, P.107

O'Barquiño is perhaps one of the best-kept secrets in el Raval. On first sight, it appears to be just another local restaurant, but go there on a Friday or Saturday night, ascend to the second floor and find yourself entering an alternate dimension: singers in drag living it up celebrating traditional Spanish song and copla. An appreciative audience often takes a break from plates of ham and glasses of wine to give an enthusiastic clap. Anyone free of prejudice is welcomed.

🕐 0900-0000 daily, Kitchen: 1300-,
Concert Jotas: 2100-0000 (F-Sa), 1900-2200 (Su)
🏠 c/Príncep de Viana, 1, el Raval
📞 +34 93 32 93 097

"Search 'O'Barquiño' in YouTube and you'll understand."
– Cristina Spanò

60 JazzSí Club

Map E, P.107

Live music fills this club every day and night. With a pedigree of over 35 years, JazzSí is part of Taller de Músics' (Musicians' Workshop) initiative to support young musicians. For a full-on journey of music, start with tributes to great jazz maestros every Monday, Cuban on Thursday, rock on Sunday and jazz or blues the rest of the time. Friday's flamenco nights are a real highlight, and start from 8.45pm. Other opening times vary from 6.30pm to 8.30pm. Admission includes first drink.

🕐 **S** *Showtime & ticket price vary with programmes* 🏠 *c/Requesens 2, el Raval*
📞 *+34 93 32 90 020*
URL *tallerdemusics.com/jazzsi-club*

"It's a small and cosy live jazz club. On Fridays it hosts flamenco nights, and it's the best flamenco you can find in Barcelona, for real."

– Soledad Arismendi

DISTRICT MAPS : **SANT ANDREU, GLÒRIES, GRÀCIA (VILA DE GRÀCIA), EL CARMEL**

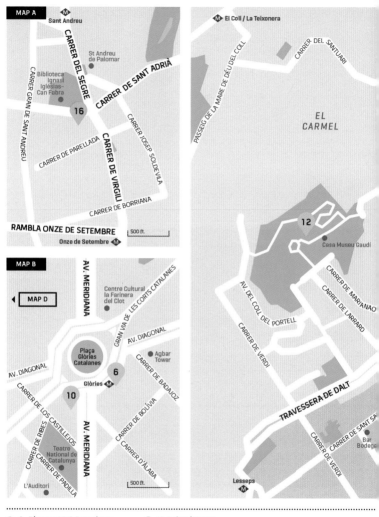

- ● 6_ Disseny HUB Barcelona
- ● 10_Els Encants Vells
- ● 12_Parc Güell
- ● 16_Fabra i Coats

MAP C

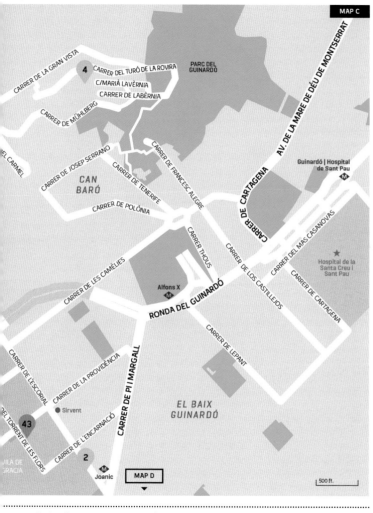

- 2_Vila de Gràcia
- 4_Bunker del Carmel
- 43_La Milagrossa Milanesa

★ Modernista building

DISTRICT MAP : GRÀCIA (VILA DE GRÀCIA), EIXAMPLE, BALMES

- 2_Vila de Gràcia
- 15_N2 Galería
- 28_SHObcn
- 29_Jazz Messengers
- 33_Kowasa
- 34_Vinçon
- 35_Colmado Quílez
- 38_La Pubilla
- 39_Bar Velódromo
- 50_Vinilo
- 56_Heliogàbal

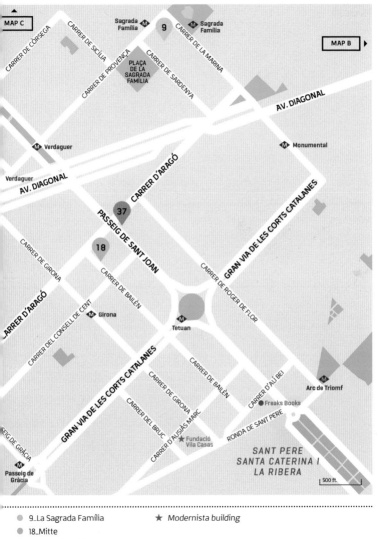

MAP C

Sagrada Família

9

Sagrada Família

CARRER DE CÒRSEGA

CARRER DE SICÍLIA

CARRER DE PROVENÇA

PLAÇA DE LA SAGRADA FAMÍLIA

CARRER DE SARDENYA

CARRER DE LA MARINA

AV. DIAGONAL

Verdaguer

Monumental

Verdaguer

AV. DIAGONAL

CARRER D'ARAGÓ

37

PASSEIG DE SANT JOAN

18

GRAN VIA LES CORTS CATALANES

CARRER DE GIRONA

CARRER DE BAILÈN

CARRER DE ROGER DE FLOR

CARRER D'ARAGÓ

CARRER DEL CONSELL DE CENT

Girona

Tetuan

CARRER DE BAILÈN

CARRER DE GIRONA

CARRER D'ALÍ BEI

Arc de Triomf

Freaks Books

CARRER DE GIRONA

CARRER DEL BRUC

CARRER D'AUSIÀS MARC

RONDA DE SANT PERE

GRAN VIA DE LES CORTS CATALANES

SEIG DE GRÀCIA

Passeig de Gràcia

Fundació Vila Casas

SANT PERE SANTA CATERINA I LA RIBERA

500 ft.

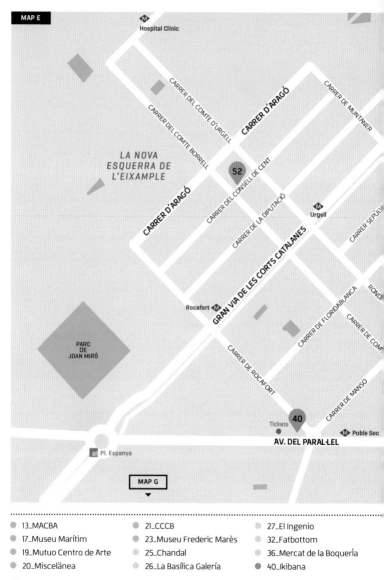

MAP E

Hospital Clínic

CARRER DEL COMTE D'URGELL

CARRER DEL COMTE BORRELL

CARRER DEL COMTE D'URGELL

CARRER D'ARAGÓ

CARRER DE MUNTANER

LA NOVA ESQUERRA DE L'EIXAMPLE

CARRER D'ARAGÓ

52

CARRER DEL CONSELL DE CENT

CARRER DE LA DIPUTACIÓ

Urgell

CARRER DEL CONSELL DE CENT

CARRER SEPÚLVEDA

CARRER D'ARAGÓ

GRAN VIA DE LES CORTS CATALANES

Rocafort

ROND

PARC DE JOAN MIRÓ

CARRER DE FLORIDABLANCA

CARRER DE COM

CARRER DE ROCAFORT

CARRER DE MANSO

Tickets

40

Poble Sec

AV. DEL PARAL·LEL

Pl. Espanya

MAP G
▼

- 13_MACBA
- 17_Museu Marítim
- 19_Mutuo Centro de Arte
- 20_Miscelànea

- 21_CCCB
- 23_Museu Frederic Marès
- 25_Chandal
- 26_La Basílica Galería

- 27_El Ingenio
- 32_Fatbottom
- 36_Mercat de la Boquería
- 40_Ikibana

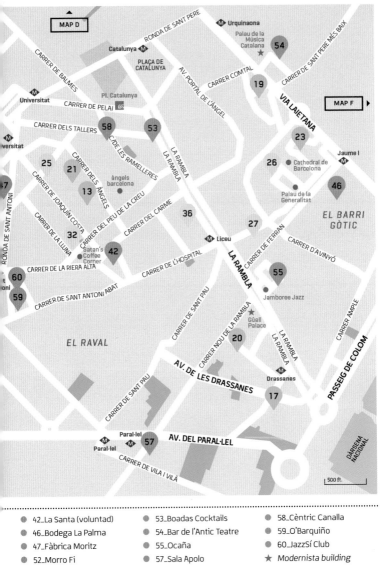

MAP D

Urquinaona

Palau de la
Música
Catalana
★ 54

RONDA DE SANT PERE

Catalunya

PLAÇA DE
CATALUNYA

CARRER DE SANT PERE MÉS BAIX

CARRER DE BALMES

AV. PORTAL DE L'ÀNGEL

CARRER COMTAL

19

VIA LAIETANA

Universitat

Pl. Catalunya

MAP F

CARRER DE PELAI

CARRER DELS TALLERS   58   53

versitat   25   21

CARRER DELS RAMELLERES

LA RAMBLA

23

CARRER DE JOAQUÍN COSTA

C/DE LES ÀNGELS

àngels
barcelona   13

26   Cathedral de
Barcelona

Jaume I

46

Palau de la
Generalitat

EL BARRI
GÒTIC

CARRER DE LA LLUNA

CARRER DEL PEU DE LA CREU   CARRER DEL CARME

36

CARRER DE LA RIERA ALTA

32   Satan's
Coffee
Corner   42

27   Liceu

CARRER DE FERRAN

CARRER D'AVINYÓ

RONDA DE SANT ANTONI

CARRER DE L'HOSPITAL

LA RAMBLA

60

CARRER DE SANT ANTONI ABAT   55

59   onl

Jamboree Jazz

EL RAVAL

CARRER DE SANT PAU

CARRER NOU DE LA RAMBLA   ★ Güell
Palace

LA RAMBLA

CARRER AMPLE

20

AV. DE LES DRASSANES

Drassanes

17

PASSEIG DE COLOM

CARRER DE SANT PAU

Paral·lel   57

Paral·lel

AV. DEL PARAL·LEL

DÀRSENA
NACIONAL

CARRER DE VILA I VILÀ

500 ft.

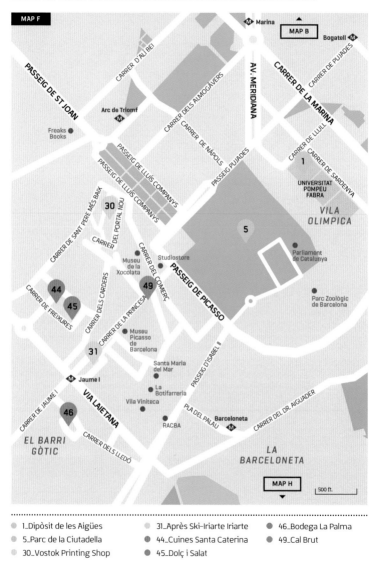

- 1_Dipòsit de les Aigües
- 5_Parc de la Ciutadella
- 30_Vostok Printing Shop
- 31_Après Ski-Iriarte Iriarte
- 44_Cuines Santa Caterina
- 45_Dolç i Salat
- 46_Bodega La Palma
- 49_Cal Brut

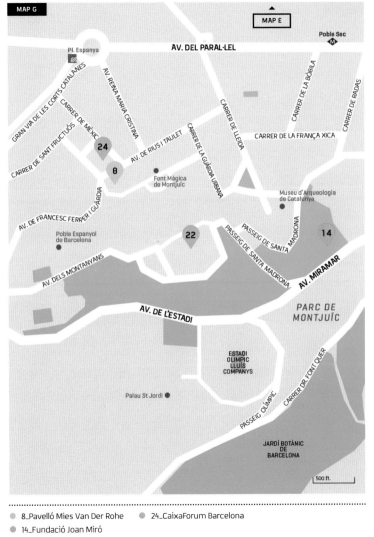

- 8_Pavelló Mies Van Der Rohe
- 14_Fundació Joan Miró
- 22_MNAC
- 24_CaixaForum Barcelona

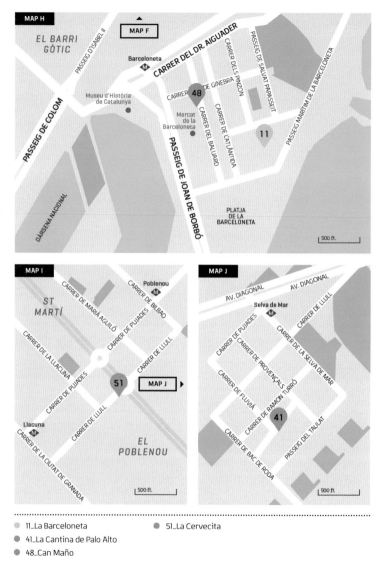

- 11_La Barceloneta
- 41_La Cantina de Palo Alto
- 48_Can Maño
- 51_La Cervecita

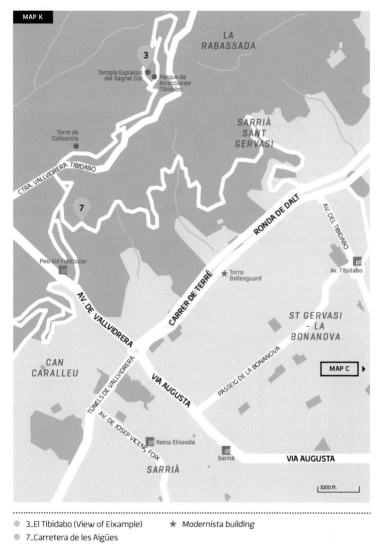

MAP K

LA RABASSADA

3 Temple Expiatori del Sagrat Cor ● Parque de Atracciones Tibidabo

SARRIÀ SANT GERVASI

Torre de Collserola

CTRA. VALLVIDRERA TIBIDABO

7

RONDA DE DALT

AV. DEL TIBIDABO

Peu del Funicular

★ Torre Bellesguard

Av. Tibidabo

AV. DE VALLVIDRERA

CARRER DE TERRÉ

ST GERVASI - LA BONANOVA

CAN CARALLEU

TÚNELS DE VALLVIDRERA

VIA AUGUSTA

PASSEIG DE LA BONANOVA

MAP C ▶

AV. DE JOSEP VICENÇ FOIX

Reina Elisenda

Sarrià

VIA AUGUSTA

SARRIÀ

1000 ft.

● 3_El Tibidabo (View of Eixample)   ★ *Modernista building*
● 7_Carretera de les Aigües

Accommodations

Hip hostels, fully-equipped apartments & swanky hotels

No journey is perfect without a good night's sleep to recharge. Whether you're backpacking or on a business trip, our picks combine top quality and convenience, whatever your budget.

 <€80   €81–200    €201+

DestinationaBCN

Comfort and style co-exist here. Twenty one- and two-bedroom pied-à-terre suites (45-120 sqm) share spectacular views of the Gothic Quarter or Eixample. Going upscale? Try the penthouse suite with private terrace. Guests can ask for anti-allergic pillows if necessary.

🏠 rda. Universitat 11, Dreta de l'Eixample
📞 +34 93 51 41 950
URL www.destinationbcn.com

El Palauet

Palauet is Catalan for "small palace," and so this is. The five-storey modernist mansion, built by Pere Falqués in 1906, houses six apartment-suites, where historic settings are partnered with modern furnishings and technology. Each suite is taken care of by a personal assistant, who can assist on meals and shopping needs.

🏠 pg. Gràcia 113, Vila de Gràcia
📞 +34 93 218 0050 URL www.elpalauet.com

Generator Hostel Barcelona

Generator is reputed to provide economy lodgings with flair. Its new Barcelona flagship goes better by adding private terraces to twin en-suite rooms. The hostel is just a ten-minute walk away from main metro stations, Diagonal and Verdaguer. Reception opens 24 hours.

 c/Còrsega 373, Vila de Gràcia
+34 93 22 00 377
URL www.generatorhostels.com

Casa Camper Barcelona

🏠 c/Elisabets 11, El Raval
☎ +34 93 34 26 280
URL www.casacamper.com

Grand Hotel Central

🏠 Vía Laietana 30, la Ribera
☎ +34 93 29 57 900
URL www.grandhotelcentral.com

Hotel OMM

🏠 c/Rosselló 265, Dreta de l'Eixample
☎ +34 93 44 54 000
URL www.hotelomm.es

Room Mate Pau

🏠 c/Fontanella 7, Dreta de l'Eixample
☎ +34 93 34 36 300
URL pau.room-matehotels.com

Notes

Index

Mark Brooks
@Mark Brooks Graphik
Design, *p083*
www.markbrooksgraphikde-
sign.com

Óscar Germade @Solo, *p094*
www.solofficial.com

P·A·R, *p062*
p-a-r.net

Pablo Rovalo
@Research Studios, *p074*
www.rsbcn.com

Pau Alekumsalaam, *p092*
www.pauerr.com

Querida, *p093*
www.querida.si

Slow, *p059*
www.slowartworks.com

Tabula Rasa Studio, *p084*
www.tabularasa.ws

Industrial

CrousCalogero, *p016*
www.crouscalogero.com

Multimedia

Bernat Fortet Unanue, *p034*
www.bernatfortet.com

Cristobal Castilla
@Aer Studio, *p054*
www.aerstudio.com

Dvein, *p045*
www.dvein.com

GIF ME, *p038*
gifme.cc

Physalia, *p098*
www.physaliastudio.com

Soledad Arismendi, *p101*
www.soledadarismendi.com
Portrait by Ana Portnoy

UnitedFakes, *p029*
www.unitedfakes.com

Publishing

David Melgarejo Vicente,
p099
twitter.com/DavidMelgarejoV

Nacho Alegre
@apartamento, *p048*
nachoalegre.com

Photo & other credits

Bar de l'Antic Teatre, *p095*
Courtesy of Bar de l'Antic Teatre

Disseny HUB Barcelona, *p019*
Courtesy of Disseny de Barcelona

Fatbottom, *p061*
Courtesy of Fatbottom

La Sagrada Família, *p022–023*
©Junta Constructora del Temple
Expiatori de la Sagrada Família

La Santa (voluntad), *p078*
Courtesy of No más – de mamá

Parc Güell, *p028–029*
Courtesy of Barcelona Serveis
Municipals, S.A.

Pavelló Mies Van Der Rohe,
p021
Courtesy of Fundació Mies Van
Der Rohe

Vostok Printing Shop, *p059*
Courtesy of Vostok Printing Shop

-
In Accommodation: all courtesy
of respective hotels

CITIX60

CITIx60: Barcelona

First published and distributed by
viction workshop ltd

viction:ary™

7C Seabright Plaza, 9-23 Shell Street,
North Point, Hong Kong

Url: www.victionary.com
Email: we@victionary.com
🅵 www.facebook.com/victionworkshop
🐦 www.twitter.com/victionary_
🅦 www.weibo.com/victionary

Edited and produced by viction:ary

Concept & art direction: Victor Cheung
Research & editorial: Queenie Ho, Caroline Kong
Project coordination: Katherine Wong, Jovan Lip
Design & map illustration: Cherie Yip

Editing: Elle Kwan
Cover map illustration: Forma & Co
Count to 10 illustrations: Guillaume Kashima aka Funny Fun
Photography: Gerard Puigmal

Content is compiled based on facts available as of February 2014. Travellers
are advised to check for updates from respective locations before your visit.

Third edition
ISBN 978-988-12227-7-0
Printed and bound in China

Acknowledgements

A special thank you to all creatives, photographer(s), editor, producers, companies and organisations for your crucial contributions to our
inspiration and knowledge necessary for the creation of this book. And,
to the many whose names are not credited but have participated in the
completion of the book, we thank you for your input and continuous
support all along.

CITIX60
City Guides

CITIx60 is a handpicked list of hot spots that illustrates the spirit of the world's most exhilarating design hubs. From what you see to where you stay, this city guide series leads you to experience the best -- the places that only passionate insiders know and go.

Each volume is a unique collaboration with local creatives from selected cities. Known for their accomplishments in fields as varied as advertising, architecture and graphics, fashion, industry and food, music and publishing, these locals are at the cutting edge of what's on and when. Whether it's a one-day stopover or a longer trip, **CITIx60** is your inspirational guide.

Stay tuned for new editions.

City guides available now:

Barcelona
Berlin
London
New York
Paris
Tokyo